Bernard of Hollywood™ PIN-UPS:

Redheads!

SUSAN BERNARD

WARNER TREASURES™

PUBLISHED BY WARNER BOOKS

A TIME WARNER COMPANY

*I have tried my very best to correctly identify
all my father's photographic subjects and apologize
if there is an error.*

Warner Books, Inc.,
1271 Avenue of the Americas
New York, NY 10020

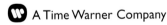 A Time Warner Company

Book design by Lisa C. McGarry

Printed in Mexico
First Printing: March 1995
10 9 8 7 6 5 4 3 2 1

ISBN: 0-446-91005-8

Most born Redheads know they're different. They take their rarity as superiority. Their lively disposition is sometimes misconstrued as hot tempered. Less than 5 percent of Americans are *born* with red hair. But, over 5 million *convert* every year. What is this urge to become a Redhead? Is it our yearning to be like the notorious flame-headed Hollywood glamour queens of times past?

Wading and rummaging through my father's abundance of files and boxes of Pin-Ups, my goal was to find the most sultry, gorgeous, coy, torrid, ravishing, impish, darling redheaded damsels ever collected. I came upon a big silver case, lined in red velvet. In it was a collection of slides, negatives and eight-by-tens of glorious russet and coral beauties. I had found rubies, copper, claret and burgundy under the golden California sun.

Even in three-quarter portraits, these feverish, fiery gamines definitely say Pin-Up! You'll see for yourself, when you turn the pages here...

Jeanne Crain

June McCall

"GOT A LIGHT?"

Unknown

"PEEKABOO"

June McCall

"SAILOR BEWARE"

Debra Paget

"MIDNIGHT LACE"

Rita Hayworth

"TENNIS ANYONE?"

June McCall

"COME HITHER"

Marilyn Hanold

"SATURDAY NIGHT"

Norma Jean/Marilyn Monroe

"BEAUTY CONTEST"

Val Njord

"JUNGLE JUNO"

Minsky Showgirl

"PRETTY IN PINK"

Marilyn Hanold

"BEAUTY IN A HAYSTACK"

Marilyn Hanold

"SUMMER DAY"

Susan Bernard

"THE AUTHOR AT WORK"

Joanne Arnold

"NET RESULT"

Renar

Tempest Storm

"ALL WRAPPED UP"

Rhonda Fleming

"WELCOME HOME!"

Marilyn Hanold

"HIDE 'N' SEEK"

Tina Louise

"WINDSWEPT"

Jeanne Crain

"CLEAR SKIES"

Val Njord

"SULTRY SIREN"

44

Val Njord

"SHIP SHAPE"

Jeanne Crain

"DOUBLE EXPOSURE"

Barbara Blaine

"SITTING PRETTY"

June McCall

"ON THE BEAM"

Monique van Vooren

"CONTEMPLATION"

Ruth Bernard-Brandeman

"AUTHOR'S MOTHER AT WORK"

Tina Louise

"SWEET DREAMS"

Many have contributed to making these publications possible: I am especially grateful to Bob Tabian, my agent, and my editor, Karen Kelly.

I owe special thanks to my assistant, Leslie Larson, and also Rod Vulich, Sygma photo agency, John Reichman, Mark Olbrich, Russell Adams, Theron Kabrich, John Gieo, London's Christie's, Ken Norwick, and my longtime legal guardian angel, Arthur Stashower.

Foremost, I am truly appreciative to my mother and father.